Lithuanian born and a music educator, she dedicated her life to teaching children the language of music. To learn the literacy of music in an easier way, I have created a lot of stories to help children to see and find relationships between the music symbol and a child's surroundings. Their inborn natural creativity and inquisition make them keen to learn new things and that was a main stimulus for me to address this book for them. I hope this book helps children to learn music in a fun and meaningful way!

Nijolé Kavaliauskaité Hunter

Little Story of Music

AUSTIN MACAULEY PUBLISHERS™
LONDON • CAMBRIDGE • NEW YORK • SHARJAH

A tribute to the memory of my aunt Laima M. from Kacergine.

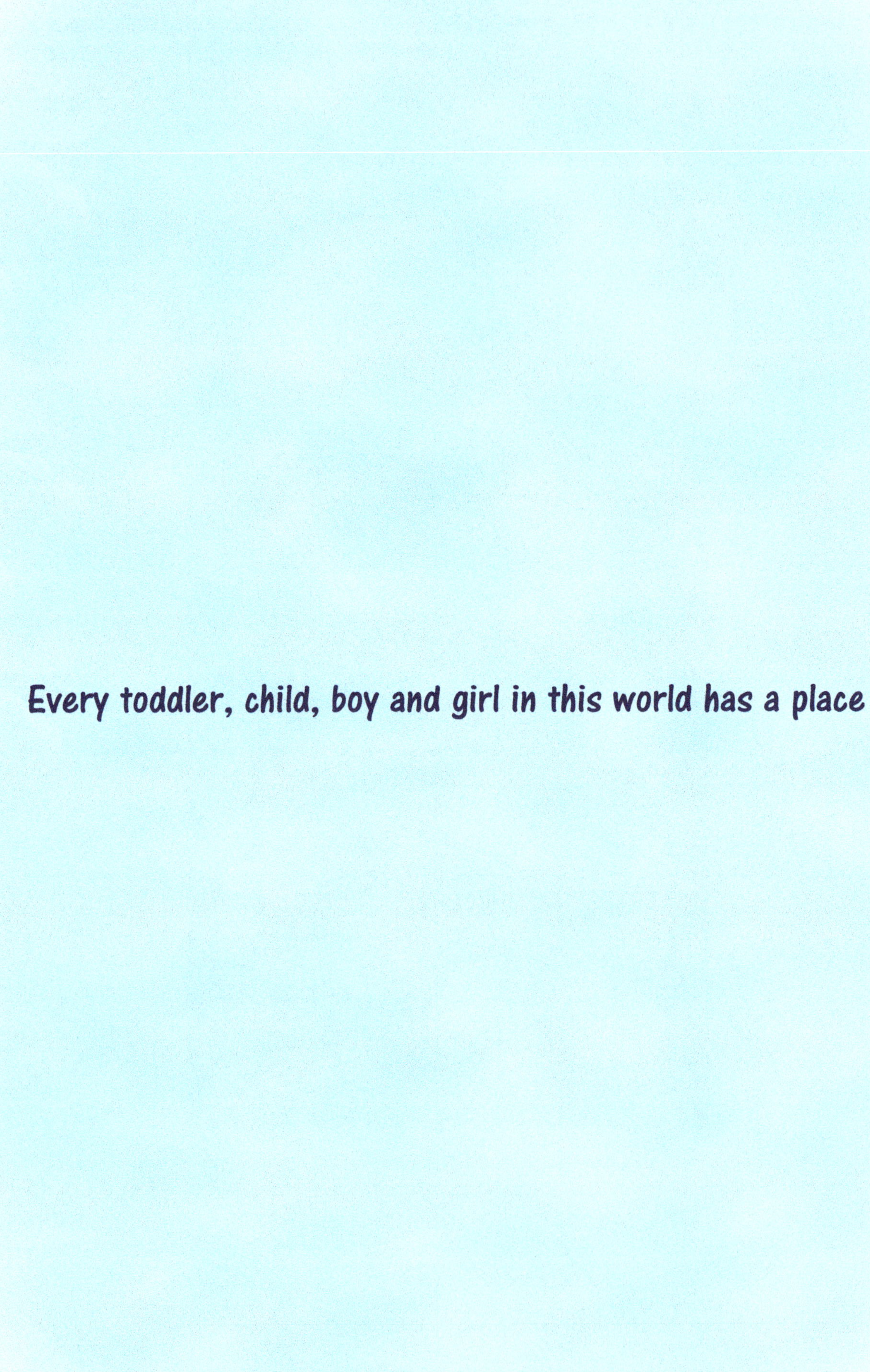

Every toddler, child, boy and girl in this world has a place

where they live with their mommy and daddy. This place is their home.

Some children live in a brick-made house and some of them live in the wooden house.
Some houses are even taller than trees, have wide windows and a chimney on the roof.
For the music notes, the house was designed using only straight horizontal lines.

5
4
3
2
1

No bricks or wood logs were needed to build it. The simplest house construction plan was used. But it came out good with everyone satisfied and that's why a birthday cake was brought.

5
4
3
2
1

For now we are a family — announced lines — with equal rights. No one is wiser or longer than others. We have one heart — that beats for us and one soul — Let's do not separate.

No matter how happy they were, the five lines felt emptiness inside. Not because there were four spaces between them, because the lines wanted to have some fun.

"Look, our cousin has visitors," exclaimed line number one.

"That's why he is so happy," said line number two.

"So, we have to invite someone to live with us," discussed line number three.

"Can we look for vegetables?" suggested line number four.

"We need to talk about it; let's meet them in person." said line number five.

But the veggies were so arrogant towards the idea to live together, that, they wouldn't leave their own garden where they grew up. Also, they liked the sun and the rain as well and have been friends with them since the veggies were born. So, the discussion to move in with the five lines did not bring any positive results.

An attempt in finding soulmates to live together with for the rest of their lives wasn't successful in spite of the five lines, who just had recently became sisters search attempts.

Then line two approached them with a new suggestion:

"Clothes? Let's invite them to join living with us, because there is a lot of space in our property for them to be happy." The lines were so sure, that, this time they would be close to the point.

So, line five, who was in the highest position, sincerely expressed to the team her thoughts, "Come on", she said sincerely.

But Mr. and Mrs. Clothes preferred to live in the wardrobe or hang on the hanger instead of choosing to live together with the lines. The offer was immediately declined.
After a while of searching, the lines chose the little dots named by notes to stay with them. But where are they now? The lines went fishing for a new friend in deep blue water.

5
4
3
2
1
?

It was a big disappointment. There was only one note swimming and it already was caught by a stranger. The lines weren't aware that the notes were not a fan of water, due to a lack of knowledge that they had never thought about regarding their unique preferences. They had been thinking mostly about their own needs. The lines did not suspect that the notes even didn't like Mr. Rain.

"Rain, rain, go away!" the notes shouted as if they saw him approaching. They knew that they could be washed out or dissolved due to rain drops.

Meanwhile, the lines did not lose their own curiosity and continued searching for friends. "Oh, maybe they are sleeping at the bottom of the lake?" discussed the lines.

And they kept looking at the water that wasn't transparent. Looking for help, the lines immediately contacted a stranger who was moving towards them.

"Have you seen one of those notes lying flat down on the bottom?" inquired the lines to the fish.

But, she was speechless. She had only two bulging eyes that looked like headlights of a car. She wiggled and wagged her tail to swim away and talked to herself.

"No, I do not want to chat with strangers," said the fish. She wasn't too friendly and preferred her species only.

The lines weren't able to find any of the notes enjoying a summer day in the field as well. "Where are they?" yelled the notes out loudly while desperately looking for friends.

At that time, the notes were homeless and did not have parents. They needed to be important to someone and be loved. For a long time they were dreaming to build a life together and begin making memories.

One day, the lines saw the notes flying out with no direction as usual. They moved through the air and had come back from a recent vacation. They had an extended period of recreation time in Mr. Trumpet's body.

5
4
3
2
1

"Look! Who is this?" the lines shouted to each other.
"Some stranger; an unknown object for us," replied one of the notes.
The notes promised to stop and get aquaintanted with the lines
personalities. And they did. Immediately the lines and the notes
became friends. It seemed that, they have known each other
for a long time.
The notes were very anxious about living together, and so, they
took a tour of their property; however, they unexpectedly became
disappointed and started mumbling out words loudly.
"There is no window to see the sun or the fall of the leaves from the
trees," sadly whispered the notes.
"There is no chimney and no fireplace to warm up when the
body is cold.
There is no winter or spring in this house — and no summer
and autumn."

"It is so boring," sadly debated the notes who expected a miracle previously. They did not have any idea, that, happiness doesn't grow on trees.

The lines realized, that, they were losing their new friends and they attempted to introduce themselves. They started to view their ongoing life historically.

"Our house," continued the notes,

"Was slowly built in a medieval age in the 13th century. At that time, the creators had been experimenting only with a straight line. And also, lines are the simplest form of any construction, because when you are looking at us, you feel quiet and rested. Equally laid out lines mean that they are in peace and harmony, and so, it means that they are in a good relationship. Medieval buildings were known as an exposition of color and light. There are some samples of previous construction that exist."

"Oh, that's an interesting story," the notes surprisingly said.

"Since the 13th century no changes have been made," continued the lines.

After clarification, the notes were finally able to realize a difference between the houses they saw flying through space and the houses located in the music country. Finally, they recognized, that, this kind of construction is a historical relic and does not have any common features with traditional constructed buildings.

"The name of our middle age residency," continued the lines, "Is a music staff."

As you see, we are five lines.
It is easy to remember just like the five fingers on both the boys and girls hands.
That's why the number of our house is 5.
Each house has a key.
To open, to enter and to live.
A special key is needed for music staff because this kind of key did not satisfy the five of us. This key was too small and invisible. We needed one to hold us tight.
During the time regarding keys many experiments have been made such as who is the initial master?
We don't know. We are sorry about that, because we would love to say to him, "Thank you." We know that just a small sample of the key is derived from the letter G.
That's the right key for us.
After the key was recognized as being useful, it has been used for many centuries until now.
It resides at the beginning of music staff.

Because the key is special, his name is a treble clef. He was recognized for his unique characteristics of being friendly and sympathetic. He wanted to be a compassionate friend to anybody sharing joy. His first goal was to settle down and second of all, to make good friends. Also, he had a vision on how a future should look like because he was born as a leader. So, looking for friends he made an announcement to all notes.

"Follow me and I will show each of you a place and give you a name. I will make you different and proud."

After his speech, the notes had trust in him, and so, decided to rely on him, lean on him, and have confidence in him.

Helped by the key, the notes entered the staff. They have been awaiting for the right instructions.

1. Never be grouchy.
2. Be friendly because we are members now.
3. Respect each other.
4. Do not copy each other to be distinguished.

The notes admired treble clef for his brave heart; they noticed that he is smarter than they were and allowed him to take the leader's position.

Treble clef said to one of the notes, "Come over and stay next to me. I am giving you a name. Do!"

And so, he replaced his other sisters and brothers in a straight line going upwards.

The notes placed in this order are expected to have a long and happy life. They looked at treble clef with a fascinating admiration.

"His unusual look reminds me of some stranger," voiced the note Do. that was met by me last summer on the green shallow grass. And not being shy at all, note Do had some courage to ask her:

"Are you treble clef's cousin?"

"Me?" said the snail — The snail was feeling like someone needed to be taught about animals.

Having the inner feeling that she might be wrong, note Do explained to snail:

"You guys are both rolled-up; so you have the same shape," note Do expressed in concern. She was young and naïve.

"Oh no," responed the snail, "I am a part of the molluscs family. I do not belong to the music world which is untouchable and doesn't have any taste. There is my story," she told them.

The snail chose to live her life on the Earth. Where she was living before, she couldn't remember. But to survive on the Earth wasn't that easy as she realized later. Her body was so small and fragile; in order to survive, she needed a pair of eyes and a home where she could be able to rest or sleep. And one day, she got two black dots, which was her eyes and a house made from shell. The snail was informed that she needs to consume a lot of calcium to make her shell harder.

After her story, things became clear to everybody's mind. For sure the snail wasn't trebble clef's cousin; she was just a very honest person. She had her own life style and enjoyed living her life as a mollusc. Musical staff needed to build his own residency because everybody already had a perfect life. There were some things that were still missing. "We need some doors!" note Fa thought when it came to a new idea. She had a slightly shy personality. In the meantime, she stepped forward tentatively to get a better look on how to go about implementing her idea.

"Let's work on it!" said note Fa.
A single view was drawn initially until the idea of having two doors came up due to safety purposes.
One thin and the other thicker — that was the best decision about their door made.
Not only for their own safety, but also a priority in this house, two doors had to be constructed. Each note deserved respect and comfort; so, for each note, a room was given separately to them. For proper separation, the bar lines was used.
They looked very straight, thin and simple.
"This project looks like a bus to me," expressed note Mi in an unusual tone to the others.
"What is a bus?" note Sol said while grimacing slightly.

And Mi had to tell everyone a story that was seen on televison. She had an inborn curiosity to things that other notes did not care about. They did remember that, a woman from the box continued to talk about how Mr. Yellow Bus loved to travel to school. He was doing his trips even when the rain was washing his chunky body or when snow and ice were creating a beautiful visual display on his windows. Actually, he looked like a house on wheels. He was seen with windows, walls and a roof. A chimney wasn't present though. Mr. Bus used his horn when he needed to communicate his own thoughts. His dictionary wasn't rich. The horn shouted as loud as he could with only one word; 'Stop'. Mr. Yellow Bus was helping children travel to the place where they could learn letters, numbers and notes of course. The children on the bus were separated by lines. The lines were thin.

If the lines would be missing, then the children could be at a great risk for contacting health problems.

And so, the lines and the notes decided to follow their sample; use a thin line. It resembled a small room. Each of us are very happy now. The house has a key, rooms, doors and is full of permanent visitors.

9 789948 259596